MW00889762

Learn Swahi

Illustrated dictionary of Kiswahili

Apprends le Swahili avec des images

Dictionnaire illustré du swahili

2024

Gusoma Publishing

Mary NJERI

Learn Shona with images by Mary NJERI

Published by Gusoma Publishing Limited
Leinster Garden, London, W2 DR, United-Kingdom.

www.gusomapublishing.com

© 2024 Gusoma Publishing

All rights reserved. No portion of this book may be reproduced in any form
without permission from the publisher, except as permitted by U.K. copyright law.

For permissions contact: contact@gusomapublishing.com

Editor : Munga SEKUNDANE

ISBN: 9798880210916

For information about special discounts available for bulk purchases, sales
promotions, fund-raising and educational needs, contact Gusoma Publishing
Company Sales at contact@gusomapublishing.com

Introduction (EN)

The book "Learn Swahili with Images" is an illustrated dictionary that helps you to memorize the vocabulary of the Swahili language.

The words are organized by topic to make learning easier. The topics cover most aspects of daily life. A section of the book is devoted to verbs in the Swahili language.

Each word in English/French has its translation in the Swahili language with an image to better understand and memorize vocabulary.

This book is easy to use and will be useful to all Swahili language learners.

This book is part of the required books program of the Mwanza School of Swahili, the Swahili language online learning school.

www.mwanzaschool.com

Munga IV SEKUNDANE, SL

Introduction (FR)

Le livre « Apprendre le swahili avec des images » est un dictionnaire illustré qui vous aide à mémoriser le vocabulaire de la langue swahili.

Les mots sont organisés par thème pour faciliter l'apprentissage. Les sujets couvrent la plupart des aspects de la vie quotidienne. Une section du livre est consacrée aux verbes en langue swahili.

Chaque mot en anglais/français a sa traduction en langue swahili avec une image pour mieux comprendre et mémoriser le vocabulaire.

Ce livre est facile à utiliser et sera utile à tous les apprenants de la langue swahili.

Ce livre fait partie du programme de livres obligatoires de la Mwanza School of Swahili, l'école d'apprentissage en ligne de la langue swahili.

www.mwanzaschool.com

Munga IV SEKUNDANE, SL

Learn Swahili online

www.mwanzaschool.com

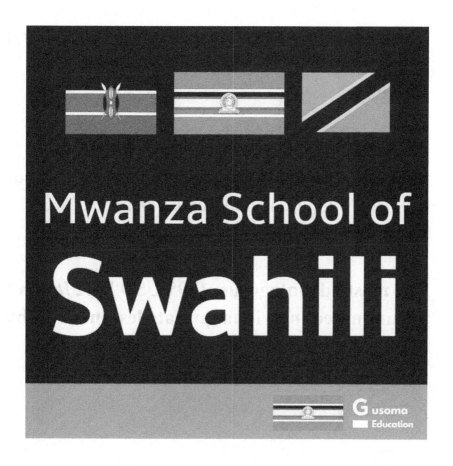

Learn Swahili online

We have several packages depending on your availability and your budget. Registration is through our website.

The most affordable: 42$ USD | €39/month for 4 hours of lessons in a group of 4 during the weekend.

The most flexible: 79$ USD | €73/month for 7 hours of individual private lessons to be booked between Wednesday and Sunday between 11:00 a.m. - 9:00 p.m.

The most advantageous: 139$ USD | €127/month for unlimited individual private lessons available every day of the week from Monday to Sunday between 8:00 a.m. - 10:00 p.m.

Learn Swahili online

Trustpilot ★★★★★ "Excellent"

from 1 hour per week

Mwanza School of Swahili

www.mwanzaschool.com

Affordable & Flexible Lessons

4 hours per month (42 USD)
7 hours per month (79 USD)
Unlimited lessons per month (139 USD)

Table of Contents

Food: Chakula, aliments

Mkate: bread, pain

Mikate: breads, pains

Maziwa: milk, lait

Mchele: rice, riz

Harage: bean, haricot

Maharage: beans, haricots

Nyama: meat, viandc

Nyama: meats, viandes

Tambi: pasta, macaroni

Tambi: pasta, macaroni

Yai: egg, **oeuf**

Mayai: eggs, **oeufs**

Samaki: fish, **poisson**

Samaki: fishes, **poissons**

Asali: honey, **miel**

Keki: cake, gâteau

Keki: cakes, gâteaux

Matunda na Mboga mboga, fruits and vegetables, fruits et légumes

Ndizi: banana, banane

Ndizi: banana, bananes

Nanasi: pineapple, ananas

Nanasi: pineapples, ananas

Kiazi mviringo: irish potato, pomme de terre

Viazi mviringo: irish potatoes, pommes de terre

Parachichi: avocado, avocat

Maparachichi: avocadoes, avocats

Embe: mango, mangue

Maembe: mangoes, mangues

Chungwa: orange, orange

Mchungwa: oranges, oranges

Limao: lemon, citron

Limao: lemons, citrons

Tufaha: apple, **pomme**

Matufaha: apples, **pommes**

Karoti: carrot, **carotte**

Karoti: carrots, **carottes**

Kitunguu: onion, **oignon**

Vitunguu: onions, **oignons**

Shule: school, école

Mwalimu: teacher, enseignant

Walimu: teachers, enseignants

Mwanafunzi: student, élève

Wanafunzi: students, élèves

Meza: table/desk, **table**

Meza: tables/desks, **tables**

Karatasi: paper, **papier**

Makaratasi: papers, **papiers**

Karamu: pen, stylo

Karamu: pens, stylos

Kitabu: book, livre

Vitabu: books, livres

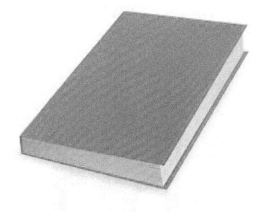

Kompyuta: computer, **ordinateur**

Kompyuta: computers,ordinateurs

Kiti: chair,**chaise**

Viti: chairs,**chaises**

Ubao: blackboard, tableau noir

Mbao: blackboards, tableaux noirs

Chaki: chalk, craie

Chaki: chalks, craies

Nguo: clothes, vêtements

Suruali: trouser, **pantalon**

Suruali: trousers, **pantalons**

Kaptura: breeche, **culotte**

Kaptura: breeches, **culottes**

Sketi: skirt, **jupe**

Sketi: skirts, **jupes**

Shati: shirt, chemise

Mashati: shirts, chemises

Gauni: dress, robe

Magauni: dresses, robes

Suruali: pants, **pantalon**

Suruali: pants, **pantalons**

Soksi: sock,**chaussette**

Soksi: socks,**chaussettes**

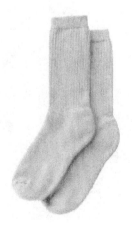

Kiatu:shoe,**chaussure**

Viatu: shoes,**chaussures**

Koti: coat, **manteau**

Makoti: coats, **manteaux**

Sweta: jumper, **pull-over**

Sweta: jumpers, **pull-overs**

Tisheti: t-shirt, **t-shirt**

Matisheti: t-shirts, **t-shirts**

Kofia: hat, chapeau

Kofia: hats, chapeaux

Masomo: subjects, cours

Sayansi: science, science

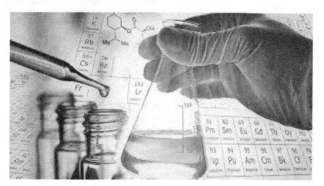

Hesabu/Hisabati: maths, mathématiques

Sanaa: arts, arts

Historia: history, histoire

Jiografia: geography, géographic

Kiingereza: english, anglais

Kusoma: **to read, lire**

Kuandika: **to write, écrire**

Afya: health, santé

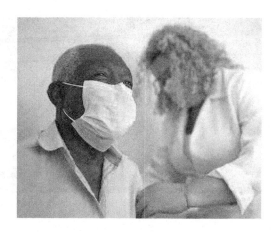

Kifaransa: french, français

Muziki: music, musique

Siku za Wiki: days of the week, jours de la semaine.

Jumatatu: monday, **lundi**

Jumanne: tuesday, **mardi**

Jumatano: wednesday, mercredi

Alhamisi: thursday, jeudi

Ijumaa: friday, **vendredi**

Jumamosi: saturday, **samedi**

Jumapili: sunday, **dimanche**

Maumbo: shapes, formes

Mraba:square, carrée

Mraba:squares, carrées

Pembe tatu: triangle, triangle

Pembe tatu: triangles, triangles

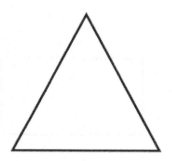

Duara: circle, **cercle**

Duara: circles, **cercles**

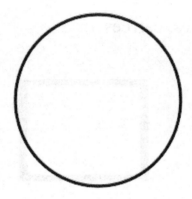

Mstatili: rectangle, **rectangle**

Mstatili: rectangles, **rectangles**

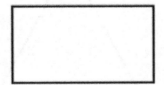

Nyota: inyenyeri

Moyo: heart, coeur

Tiara, kite, **cerf-volant**

Tiara, kites, **cerf-volants**

Mviringo: oval, **ovale**

Mviringo: ovals, **ovales**

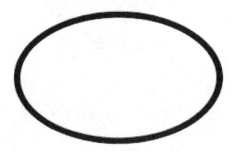

Pembe sita: hexagon, **hexagone**

Pembe sita: hexagons, **hexagones**

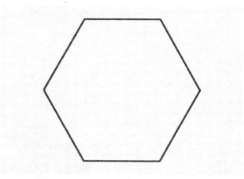

Pembe tano: pentagon, **pentagone**

Pembetano: pentagons, **pentagones**

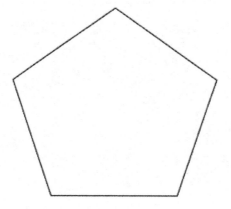

Hali ya Hewa: weather, météo

Jua: sun, soleil

Wingu: cloud, nuage

Mawingu: clouds, nuages

Mvua: rain, pluie

Mvua: rains, pluies

Upepo: wind, vent

Pepo: winds, vents

Dhoruba: storm, tempête

Dhoruba: storms, tempêtes

Radi: thunder/lightning, tonnerre/ éclair

Radi: thunders/lightnings, tonnerres/ éclairs

Theluji: snow, **neige**

Theluji: snows, **neiges**

Mvua ya mawe: hail, **grêle**

Upinde wa mvua: rainbow, **arc en ciel**

Upinde wa mvua: rainbows, **arcs en ciel**

Rangi: colours, **couleurs**

Nyekundu: red, **rouge**

Njano/Manjano: yellow, **jaune**

Kijani: green, vert

Bluu: blue, bleu

Rangi ya chungwa: orange, orangc

Rangi ya waridi/Pinki: pink, rose

Zambarau: purple, **mauve**

Nyeusi: black, **noir**

Kahawia: brown, **marron**

Nyeupe: white, **blanc**

Miezi ya mwaka: months of the year, mois de l'année

Januari/Mwezi wa kwanza: january, janvier

Februari/Mwezi wa pili: february, février

Machi/Mwezi wa tatu: march: **mars**

Aprili/Mwezi wa nne: april, **avril**

Mei/Mwezi wa tano: may, mai

Juni/Mwezi wa sita: june, juin

Julai/Mwezi wa saba: july, **juillet**

Agosti/Mwezi wa nane: **august, août**

Septemba/Mwezi wa tisa: **september, septembre**

Oktoba/Mwezi wa kumi: october, **octobre**

Novemba/Mwezi wa kumi na moja: november, novembre

Disemba/Mwezi wa kumi na mbili: december, décembre

Namba: numbers, nombres

Moja: one, un

Mbili: two, deux

Tatu: three, trois

Nne: four, quatre

Tano: five, cinq

Sita: six, six

Saba: seven, sept

Nane: eight:, huit

Tisa: nine, neuf

shutterstock.com · 1178341768

Kumi: ten, dix

Mifugo: farm animals, animaux de la ferme

Ng'ombe: cow, vache

Ng'ombe: cows, vaches

Nguruwe: pig, cochon

Nguruwe: pigs, cochons

Kondoo: sheep, mouton

Kondoo: sheeps, moutons

Kuku: chicken, poulet

Kuku: chickens, poulets

Farasi: horse, cheval

Farasi: horses, chevaux

Mbuzi: goat, chèvre

Mbuzi: Goats, chèvres

Mbwa: dog, chien

Mbwa: dogs, chiens

Paka: cat, chat

Paka: cats, chats

Bata: duck, canard

Bata: ducks, canards

Bata bukini: goose, oie

Bata bukini: gooses, oies

Wanyama wa Kiafrika: african animals, animaux africains

Simba: lion, lion

Simba: lions, lions

Tembo: elephant, éléphant

Tembo: elephants, éléphants

Twiga: giraffe, **girafe**

Twiga: giraffes, **girafes**

Nyani: chimpanzee, **chimpanzé**

Nyani: chimpanzees, **chimpanzés**

Sokwe: gorilla, gorille

Sokwe: gorillas, gorilles

Pundamilia: zebra, zèbre

Pundamilia: zebras, zèbres

Mamba: crocodile, **crocodile**

Mamba: crocodiles, **crocodiles**

Kiboko: hippopotamus: **hippopotame**

Kiboko: hippopotamus: **hippopotames**

Kifaru: rhinoceros, **rhinocéros**

Kifaru: rhinoceros, **rhinocéros**

Tai: vulture, **vautour**

Tai: vultures, **vautours**

Watu wanaotusaidia: people who help us, gens qui nous aident

Daktari: doctor, docteur

Madaktari: doctors, docteurs

Nesi: nurse, infirmier

Manesi: nurses, infirmiers

Polisi/Askari: policeman/woman, **policier/ policière**

Mapolisi/Maaskari: policemen/women, **policiers/ policières**

Mwalimu: teacher, **enseignant**

Walimu: teachers, **enseignants**

Dakari wa mifugo: vet , vétérinaire

Madaktari wa mifugo   : vets , vétérinaires

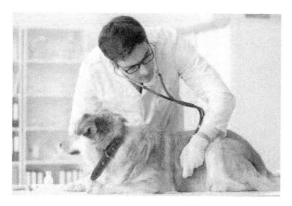

Mkulima: Farmer, Cultivateur

Wakulima: Farmers, cultivateurs

Padri/Mtumishi wa Mungu: priest, **prêtre**

Mapadri/Watumishi wa Mungu: priests, **prêtres**

Mpishi: cook, **cuisinier**

Wapishi: cooks, **cuisiniers**

Mama: mother, mère

Baba: father, père

Bibi/Nyanya: grandmother, **grand-mère**

Babu: grandfather, **grand-père**

Mwili: body, corps

Mkono: arm, bras

Mikono: arms: bras

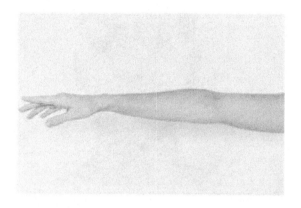

Mguu: leg, jambe

Miguu: legs, jambes

Kichwa: head, tête

Vichwa: heads, têtes

Jicho: eye, oeil

Macho: eyes, yeux

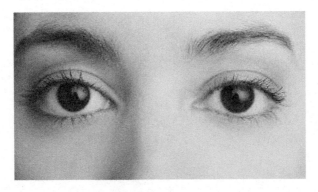

Pua: nose, nez

Pua: nose, nez

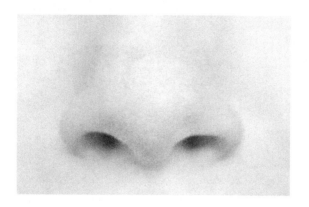

Sikio: ear, oreille

Masikio

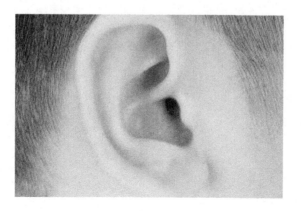

Kinywa: mouth, **bouche**

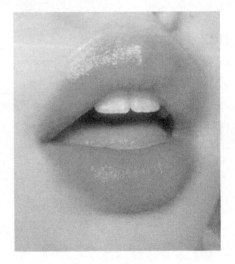

Kiganja: hand, **main**

Viganja: hands, **mains**

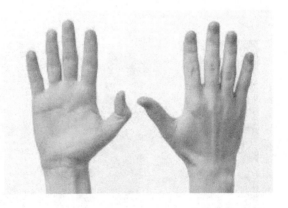

Kidole: finger, doigt

Vidole: fingers, doigts

Mguu: foot, pied

Miguu: feet, pieds

Kucha: toe, doigt de pied

Kucha: toes , orteils

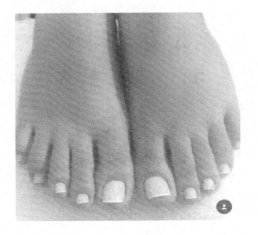

Goti: knee, genou

Magoti: knees, genoux

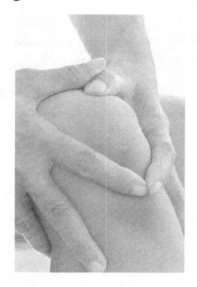

Bega: shoulder, épaule

Mabega: shoulders , épaules

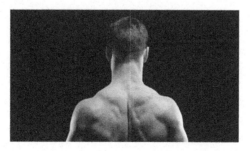

Kiwiko/Viwiko: elbows , coudes

Shingo: neck, cou

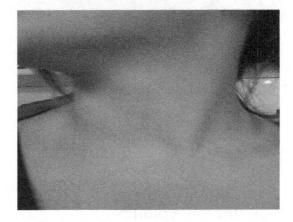

Nywele: hair, cheveux

Jino: tooth, dent

Meno: teeth, dents

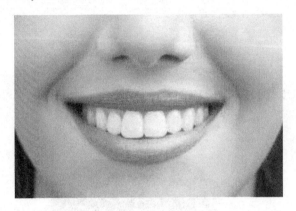

Kidevu: chin, menton

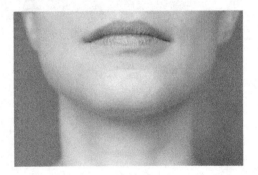

Kufanya kazi: to work, **travailler**

Kuzungumza/Kuongea:to talk, **parler**

Kusema/Kuambia: **to tell, dire**

Kuondoka: **to leave, aller**

Kwenda:to go, aller

Kupata: to get, avoir

Kujua: to know, **savoir**

Kufikiria: to think, **penser**

Kuchukua: to take, prendre

Kuona: to see, voir

Kuangalia: to watch, Voir

Kuja: to come, venir

Kutaka: to want, vouloir

Kutafuta: to seek, chercher

Kutumia: to use, **utiliser**

Kupa/Kugawa: to give, **donner**

Kupiga: to call, **appeler**

Kujaribu: to try, **essayer**

Kuuliza: to ask, **demander**

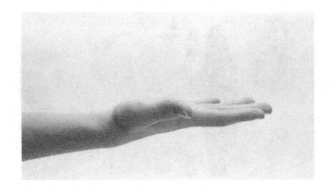

Kuomba: to request, **demander**

Kuhitaji: to need, besoin

Kulazimika: to must, devoir

Kuhisi: to feel, sentir

Kutoka: to exit, quitter

Kutelekeza: to abandon, **abandonner**

Kuweka: to put, **mettre**

Kumaanisha: **to mean, signifier**

Kutunza: **to keep, conserver**

Kuruhusu: to allow, autoriser

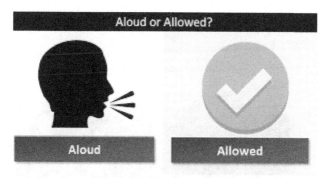

Kuanza: to start, commencer

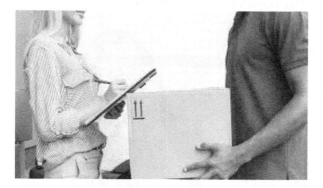

Kuanza: to begin, **commencer**

Kuonekana: to seem, **sembler**

Kusaidia: to help, aider

Kuokoa: to save, sauve

Kujadili: to discuss, discuter

Kugeuka: to turn, tourner

Kuonesha/Kuonyesha: to show, **montrer**

Kusikia: to hear, entendre

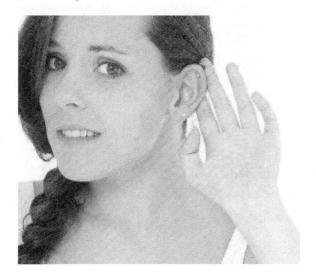

Kucheza: **to play, jouer**

Kukimbia: **to run, courir**

Kusogea: to move, bouger

Kuvutiwa/Kupenda: to like, aimer

Kuishi: to live, vivre

Kuamini: to believe, croire

Kushikilia/Kushika/Kubeba: to hold, tenir

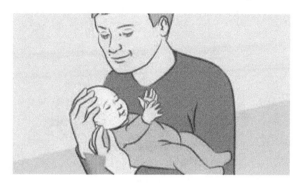

Kuleta: to bring, apporter

Kutokea: to happen, Être

Kuandika: to write, écrire

Kuhudumia: to provide, fournir

Kukaa: to sit, s'asseoir

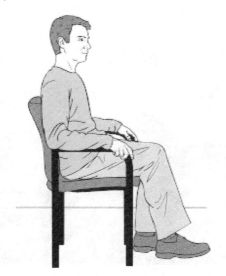

Kusimama: to stand, se mettre debout

Kupoteza: to lose: perdre

Kulipa: to pay, **payer**

Kukutana: to meet, **rencontrer**

Kuongezeka: to increase, augmenter

Kuendelea: to continue, continuer

Kupanga: to set, poser

Kujifunza: to learn, étudier

Kubadilika: to change, **changer**

Kuongoza:to lead, **diriger**

Kuuelewa: to understand, comprendre

Kufuata:to follow, suivre

Kuacha/Kuzuia: **to stop, arrêter**

Kutengeneza/Kuumba: **to create, créer**

Kuzungumza/Kuongea: to speak, parler

Kusoma: to read, lire

Kujumlisha/Kuongeza: to add, ajouter

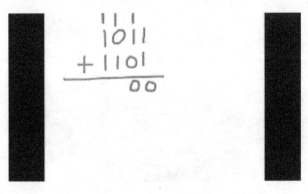

Kutumia: to spend, dépenser

Kukua/Kuotesha/Kuota: **to grow, grandir**

Kufungua: **to open, ouvrir**

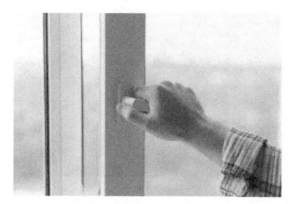

Kutembea: to walk, **marcher**

Kushinda: to win, **gagner**

Kutoa: to offer, offrir

Kukumbuka: to remember, se souvenir

Kupenda: to love, aimer

Kufikiria/Kuwaza: to consider, considérer

Kutokea: to appear, apparaître

Kununua: to buy, acheter

Kuuza, to sell, **vendre**

Kusubiri: to wait, **attendre**

Kuhudumia: to serve, servir

Kufa/Kufariki: to die, mourir

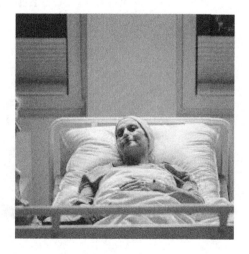

Kutuma: to send, envoyer

Kutarajia/Kutegemea : to expect, attendre

Kujenga: to build, **construire**

Kubaki: to stay, **rester**

Kuanguka: **to fall, tomber**

Kukata: **to cut, couper**

Kufika: to reach, **arriver**

Kuua: to kill, **tuer**

Kusalia: to remain, **rester**

Kupendekeza: to suggest, **suggérer**

Kuinua/Kukuza: to raise, élever

Kupita/Kushinda: to pass, passer

Kupasa/Kutaka: to require, exiger

Kukabidhi: to hand over, remettre

Kuamua: to decide, **décider**

Kuvuta: to pull, **tirer**

Safiri: travel, voyage

Safari/Safiri: journey, voyage

Safari: journey, voyages

Gari: car, voiture

Magari/gari: cars, voitures

Basi: bus, autobus

Mabasi: buses, autobus

Gari moshi: train, train

Gari moshi: trains, trains

Ndege: airplane, **avion**

Ndege: airplanes, **avions**

Egesho la magari: taxi park, **parc de taxi**

Maegesho ya magari: taxi parks, **parcs des taxis**

Uwanja wa ndege: airport, **aéroport**

Viwanja vya ndege: airports, **aéroports**

Kuondoka: to take off, **décoller,**

Abiria: passenger, passager

Abiria: passengers, passagers

Njia/Barabara: route, rue

Njia/Barabara: routes, rues

Barabara: road, **route**

Barabara: roads, **routes**

Likizo: vacation, **vacances**

Likizo: vacations, **vacances**

Baiskeli: bicycle, vélo

Baiskeli: bicycles, vélos

Pikipiki: motorcycle, moto

Pikipiki: motorcycles, motos

Meli/Mashua: ship/ boat, **bateau,**

Meli/Mashua: ships/ boats, **bateaux,**

Vyanzo vya Maji: water bodies, eau

Mto: river, rivière

Mito: rivers, rivières

Bahari: sea, mer

Bahari: seas, mers

Bahari : ocean, océan

Bahari: oceans, océans

Kisiwa, island, île

Visiwa, islands, îles

Ghuba: gulf, **golfe**

Ghuba: gulfs, **golfes**

Mfereji: canal, **canal**

Mifereji: canals, **canaux**

Ziwa: lake, lac

Maziwa: lakes, lacs

Maporomoko ya maji: waterfall, cascade

Maporomoko ya maji: waterfalls, cascades

Bandari: port, **port**

Bandari: ports, **ports**

Mkondo: stream, **ruisseau**

Mikondo: streams, **ruisseaux**

Chanzo: source, source

Vyanzo: sources, sources

Misimu ya Mwaka: seasons of the year, saisons de l'année

Masika: spring, **printemps**

Kiangazi: **summer**, été

Kipupwe: winter, hiver

Demani: autumn, automne

Wadudu: insects, insectes

Inzi: fly, mouche

Nzi: flies, mouches

Kipepeo: butterfly, papillon

Vipepeo: butterflies, papillons

Panzi: grasshopper, **sauterelle**

Panzi: grasshoppers, **sauterelles**

Mchwa: ant, **fourmi**

Mchwa: ants, **fourmis**

Nyuki: bee, abeille

Nyuki: bees, abeilles

Mbu: mosquito, moustique

Mbu: mosquitoes, moustiques

Kiwavi: caterpillar, chenille

Viwavi: caterpillars, chenilles

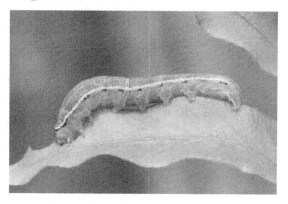

Buibui: spider, araignée

Buibui: spiders, araignées

Mende: cockroach, **cafard**

Mende: cockroaches, **cafards**

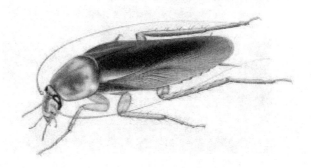

Mdudu wa udongo: earthworm, **ver de terre**

Wadudu wa udongo, earthworms, **vers de terre**

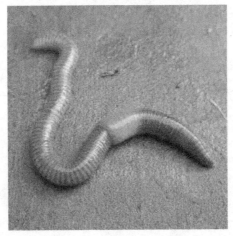

Nyigu: wasp, **guêpe**

Nyigu: wasps, **guêpes**

Michezo: sport, sport

Uwanja: arena, stade de l'aréna

Viwanja: arenas, stade de l'aréna

Mwanariadha: athlete, athlète

Wanariadha: athletes , athlètes

Nahodha/Kapteni: captain, **capitaine**

Manahodha/Makapteni: captains, **capitaines**

Kocha: coach,entraîneur

Makocha: coaches, entraîneurs

Ushindani: competition, competition

Mashindano: competitions, compétitions

Kombe: cup, coupe

Makombe: cups, coupes

Kushinda: to defeat, vaincre

Kutetea: to defend, defendre

Shabiki: fan, ventilateur

Mashabiki: fans, ventilateurs

Uwanja: field, terrain

Viwanja: fields, terrains

Kuchora/Chora: **draw, match nul**

Gori: **goal, but**

Magori: **goals, buts**

Mapumziko: half time, mi-temps

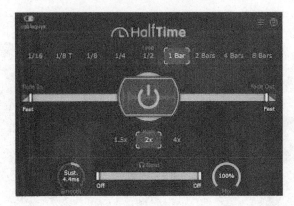

Kuotea: offside, hors-jeu

Penaliti: penalty, pénalité

Penaliti: penalties, pénalités

Mchezaji: player, joueur

Wachezaji: players, joueurs

Shuti: **shoot, tir**

Mashuti: **shoots, tirs**

Sheria: rules, règle

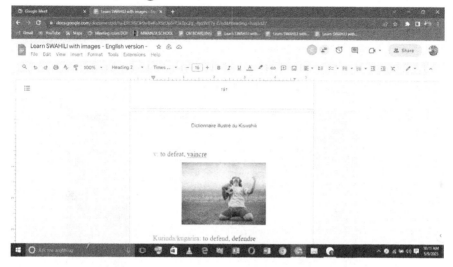

Sheria: rules, règlement

Mwamuzi: referee, **arbitre**

Waamuzi: referees, **arbitres**

Nyara/Kombe: trophy, **trophée**

Nyara/Makombe: trophies, **trophées**

Filimbi: whistle, sifflet

Filimbi: whistles, sifflets

Ushindi: victory, victoire

Rekodi: **record, résultat**

Mpira wa miguu: **football, football**

Mpira wa wavu: volleyball, volley-ball

Mpira wa kikapu: basketball, basket-ball

Mpira wa kikapu: basketball, basket-ball

Ndondi: **boxing, boxe**

Familia: family, famille

Mama mdogo/Mama mkubwa: aunt(maternal),tante maternelle

Mama wadogo/Mama wakubwa: aunts(maternal),tantes maternelle

Mjomba (maternal), data wacu, Baba mdogo/ Baba mkubwa (paternal): uncle, oncle

Wajomba(maternal), data wacu, Baba wadogo/Wakubwa (paternal): uncles, oncles

Ndugu: sibling, **frère/ soeur**

Ndugu: siblings, **frères/ soeurs**

Mzazi: parent, **parent**

Ababyeyi: parents, **parents**

Mvulana /Mkubwa/Kaka (for boys): brother, frère

Wavulana/Wakubwa/Kaka/Makaka (for boys): brothers, frères

Msichana/ Mkubwa/ Dada: sister, (for girls), soeur

Wasichana/ Wakubwa/ Dada/Madada: sisters, (for girls), soeurs

Binamu: cousin, cousin

Binamu: cousins, cousins

Mume: husband, mari

Waume: husbands, maris

Mkc/Muke: wife, femme

Wake: wives, femmes

Mtoto: child, enfant

Watoto: children, enfants

Mjukuu: grandchild, **petit-fils**

Wajukuu: grandchildren, **petits-enfants**

Mama wa kambo: stepmother, **belle-mère**

Mama wa kambo: stepmothers, **belle-mères**

Mkwe: in-law, beau-parent

Wakwe: in-laws, beaux-parents

Mwana/ Mtoto wa kiume: son, fils

Wana/ watoto wa kiume: sons, fils

Umuhungu

Mwana/ Mtoto wa kike: **daughter, fille**

Wana/ Watoto wa kike: **daughters, filles**

Ajira: employment, emploi

Ziada: bonus, bonus

Wasifu: curriculum vitae, curriculum vitae

Wasifu: curriculum vitae, curriculum vitae

Ondoa/Fukuza: to dismiss, **congédier**

Mwajiri: employer, **employeur**

Waajiri: employers, **employeurs**

Kufukuza: to fire, virer

Mahojiano/Hoji: interview, interview

Likizo ya uzazi: maternity leave, congé de maternité

Kukuza/Kupandisha cheo: promotion: promotion

Kuajiri : to recruit, recruteur

Kustaafu: to retire, partir à la retraite

Kujiuzulu: to resign, démissionner

Mshahara: salary, salaire

Mishahara: salaries, salaires

Mwajiriwa: staff, employee

Waajiriwa: staff, employees

Sheria: law, droit

Wakili: attorney, avocat

Mwendesha mashtaka: prosecutor, procureur

Waendesha mashtaka: prosecutors, procureurs

Uamuzi: verdict, **verdict**

Maamuzi: verdicts, **verdicts**

Kesi: case, **cas**

Kesi: cases, **cas**

Kushtaki: to sue, poursuivre en justice

Mkataba: contract, contrat

Mahakama ya sheria: court of law, **tribunal**

Mahakama za sheria: courts of law, **tribunaux**

Ushahidi: evidence, **preuve**

Shahidi: evidences, **preuves**

Hatia: guilty, coupable

Hakimu: judge, juge

Mahakimu: judges, juges

Baraza la waamuzi: jury, **jury**

Mwanasheria: lawyer, avocat

Wanasheria: lawyers, avocats

Hukumu: sentence, peine

Benki, bank, banque

Salio: balance, solde

Xero Today's Bank Balance

Account: Business Bank Account

$1,760.54

Closing Balance

Makato ya benki: bank charges, frais bancaires

Charges	Fund transfers - NEFT, RTGS, IMPS	ECS / cheque return	SMS alerts	Debit card PIN reset (offline)	Duplicate statement
ICICI Bank	Rs 2.50-50 per transaction	Rs 350 for first return in a month, thereafter Rs 750 per return in the same month	Rs 15 per quarter	Rs 25	Rs 50-100 per statement
HDFC Bank	Rs 2.50-50 per transaction	Rs 350 for first return in a quarter, thereafter Rs 750 per return in same quarter	Rs 15 per quarter	Rs 50	Rs 50-100 per statement
SBI	Rs 2-45 per transaction	Rs 150-500	Rs 15 per quarter	Rs 50	Rs 50-100 per passbook
Axis Bank	Rs 2.50-Rs 50 per transaction	Rs 350 for first return, thereafter Rs 750 per return in the same month	Rs 5 per month	Rs 100	Rs 100
Kotak Mahindra Bank	Nil-Rs 50 per transaction	Rs 500 per instance	Rs 15-30 per quarter	Rs 100	Rs 100 per request

Tawi: branch, **branche**

Matawi: branches, **branches**

Kitabu cha hundi: checkbook, **chéquier**

Vitabu vya hundi: checkbooks, **chéquiers**

Cheki: check, chèque

Cheki: checks, chèques

Mkopo: credit, crédit

Mikopo: credits, crédits

Kadi ya benki: bank card, **carte de retrait**

Kadi za benki: bank cards, **cartes de retrait**

Akaunti ya sasa: current account, **compte courant**

Akaunti za sasa: current accounts, **comptes courant**

in million US Dollar

Items	FY04	FY05	FY06	Yr to Yr change FY06
1. Trade balance	-1,279	-4,514	-8,442	-3,928
Exports	12,459	14,482	16,506	2,024
Imports	13,738	18,996	24,948	5,952
2.Services (net)	-1,316	-3,293	-4,402	-1,109
Transportation	-890	-1218	-1790	-572
Travel	-1034	-995	-1,185	-190
Communication services	166	272	97	-175
Other business services	-382	-2,217	-2,552	-335
Government services	905	1,041	1,359	318
Other	-131	-176	-331	-155
3.Investment Income (net)	-2,207	-2,386	-2,671	-285
Direct investment	-1,215	-1,622	-2,076	-454
Portfolio investment	-201	-154	-95	59
Interest Payments on Official and Private External Debt	-839	-764	-749	15
Others	48	154	249	95
4. Current transfers (net)	6,814	8,659	10,516	1,857

Deni: debit, débit

Account Name	Debit	Credit
Cash	1,000	
Accounts Receivable		1,000

AKaunti ya kutunzia: saving account, compte épargne

Akaunti za kutunzia: saving accounts, compte épargne

Kuweka/Kujaza: to fill in, compléter

Hisa/riba: interest, intérêt

Hisa/riba: interests, intérêts

Mkopo: loan, crédit

Mikopo: loans, crédits

Mlipaji: payee, bénéficiaire

Walipaji: payees, bénéficiaires

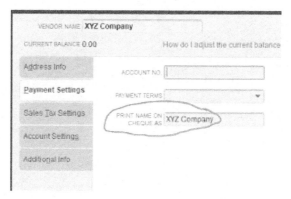

Kutoa: withdraw, retirer

Mauzo: sales, ventes

Mnunuzi: buyer, acheteur/ acheteuse

Wanunuzi: buyers, acheteurs/ acheteuses

Mteja: customer, client

Wateja: customers, clients

Punguzo: **discount, réduit**

Fuatilia: follow up, **suivi**

Dhamana: guarantee, **garantie**

Bidhaa: product, **produit**

Bidhaa: products, **produits**

Huduma: service, service

Huduma: services, services

Kwa wingii: in bulk, en gros

Baada ya huduma ya mauzo: **after sale service, service après-vente :**

Baada ya huduma za mauzo: **after sales services, services après-vente :**

Sikukuu na Sherehe/Karamu: fêtes et fêtes, holidays and feasts

Mwaka mpya: new year, nouvel an

Noëli/Krismasi: christmas, noël

Pasaka: easter, pâques

Ubatizo: baptism, baptême

Harusi: wedding, **mariage**

Harusi: weddings, **mariages**

Siku ya Mashujaa: heroes day, **journée des héros**

Siku ya kuzaliwa: birthday, **anniversaire**

Siku za kuzaliwa: birthdays, **anniversaires**

Jumapili ya Matawi/Mitende: palm Sunday, **dimanche des rameaux**

Siku ya wafanyakazi: labour's day, fête du travail

Ukumbusho: commemoration, commémoration

Mikutano: meetings, réunions

Anwani: address, adresse

Anwani: addresses, adresses

Kutokuwepo/ hayupo: absent, absent

Kufikia: to achieve, **accomplir**

Kuahirisha: to adjourn, ajourner

Mkutano mkuu wa mwaka : AGM, réunion annuelle

Mzungumzaji mgeni : guest speaker, conférencier

Wazungumzaji wageni : guest speakers, conférenciers

Kuchemsha bongo: to brainstorm, réfléchir ensemble

Mwenyekiti: chairperson, président

Wenyekiti: chairpersons, présidents

Ajenda: agenda, ordre du jour

Mshiriki: participant, participant

Washiriki: participants, participants

Chumba cha bodi: **boardroom, salle**

Vyumba vya bodi: **boardrooms, salles**

Makubaliano: **consensus, unanimité**

Kushirikiana: collaborate, collaborer

Mkutano: conference, conférence

Mikutano: conferences, conférences

Lazima: mandatory, obligatoire

Lazima: mandatories, obligatoires

Lengo: objective, objectif

Malengo: objectives, objectifs

Kunyoosha mkono: show of hand, montrer le main

Kunyoosha mikono: show of hands, montrer les mains

Vyumba ndani ya nyumba: rooms in a house, chambres dans une maison

Dari: attic, grenier

Dari: attics, greniers

Ghorofa ya chini: basement, sous-sol

Ghorofa za chini: basement, sous-sol

Bafu: bathroom, salle de bain

Mabafu: bathrooms, salles de bain

Chumba cha kulala: bedroom, chambre à coucher

Vyumba vya kulala bedrooms, chambres à coucher

Korido/Barabara ya ukumbini: hallway, corridor

Korido/ Barabara za kumbini: hallways, corridors

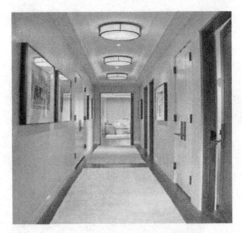

Chumba cha kulia: dining room, salle à manger

Vyumba vya kulia: dining rooms, salles à manger

Jiko: kitchen, cuisine

Majiko: kitchens, cuisines

Sebule: living room, saloon

Sebule: living rooms, saloons

Chumba kamili: master room, **chambre principale**

Vyumba kamili: master rooms, **chambres principales**

Samani na Mapambo: furniture and decor, meubles et décor

Kitanda: bed, lit

Vitanda: beds, lits

Kabati: cupboard, armoire

Kabati: cupboards, armoires

Kioo, mirror, **miroir**

Vioo, mirrors, **miroirs**

Sofa: sofa, **divan**

Sofa: sofas, **divans**

Picha: picture, image

Picha, pictures, images

Vyombo vya Nyumbani: household appliances, appareils ménagers

Friji: fridge, frigo

Friji: fridges, frigos

Tanuri: oven, four

Tanuri: ovens, fours

Jiko: stove, cuisinière

Majiko: stoves, cuisinières

Vifaa vya usafi/kusafisha: cleaning supplies, fournitures de nettoyage

Ufagio: broom, balai

Mifagio: brooms, balais

Dekio/deki: **mop, lavette**

Madekio/deki: **mops, lavettes**

Kufua: laundry, linge et lessive

Pasi: clothing iron, fer à repasser

Pasi: clothing irons, fers à repasser

Shuka: sheet, drap

Mashuka: sheets, draps

Kufua/Kufulia: laundry, laver

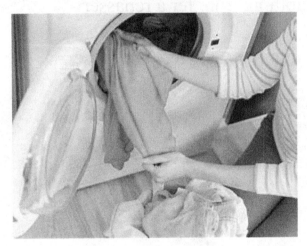

Maneno ya kufafanua kwa wafanyakazi wa ndani: describing words for housekeepers, description des mots pour les femmes de ménage

Safisha: clean, nettoyer

Vumbi: dusty, poussiéreux

Lowa/lowanisha/mvua: wet, mouillé

Lowa/lowanisha/mvua: wet, mouillé

Fujo: messy, désordonné

Maneno ya vitendo kwa wafanyakazi wa ndani: paroles d'action pour les femmes de ménage, action words for housekeepers

Kusafisha: to clean, nettoyer

Kumwagilia: to water, arroser

Kupanga: to organize, organiser

Kufuta: to wipe, essuyer

Kuosha: to wash, laver

Kudeki: to mop, torcher

Kupiga simu: to call, **téléphoner**

Shughuli/Bizi: busy, **occupé**

Laini ya simu: SIM card, carte SIM

Laini za simu: SIM cards, Cartes SIM

Ujumbe mfupi: text, SMS

Matibabu: medical, médical

Isiyo ya kawaida/Kichaa: abnormal, anormal

Wasio wa kawaida/ Vichaa: abnormals, anormaux

Gari la wagonjwa: ambulance, ambulance

Magari ya wagonjwa: ambulances, ambulances

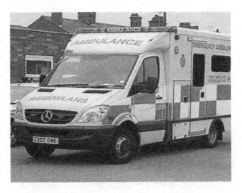

Usahaulifu: amnesia, amnésie

Antibiotiki/kiuavijasumu/dawa ya kutuliza maumivu: antibiotic, **antibiotique**

Antibiotiki/Viuavijasumu/Dawa za kutuliza maumivu: antibiotics, **antibiotiques**

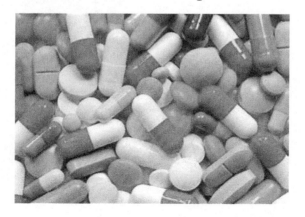

Mkutano: appointment, rendez-vous

Mikutano: appointments rendez-vous

Pumu: asthma, asthme

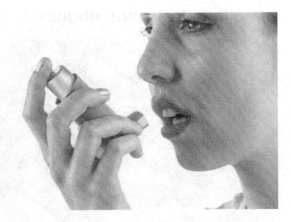

Kidonda: bedsore, escarre

Vidonda: bedsores, escarres

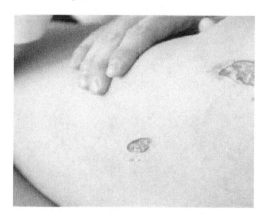

Shinikizo la damu: blood pressure, tension artérielle

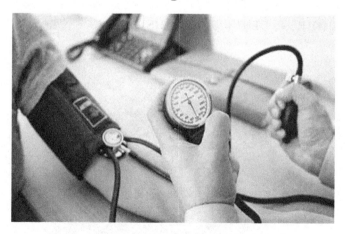

Vunjika: **broken, cassé**

Mchubuko: **bruise, contusion**

Michubuko: **bruises, contusions**

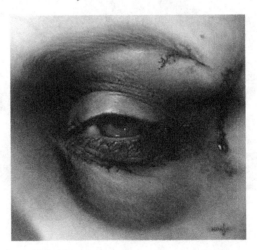

Kiziwi: deaf, sourd

Viziwi: deafs, sourds

Kuvunjika/vunjika: fracture, fracture

Kuvunjika/Vunjika: fractures, fractures

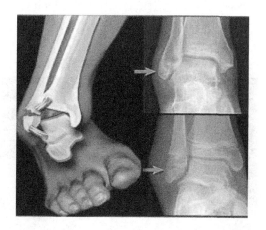

Mshipa: IV, IV

Mishipa: IV, IV

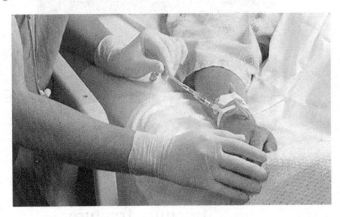

Kichanga/Mtoto mchanga: newborn, **nouveau-né**

Vichanga/Watoto wachanga: newborns, **nouveau-nés**

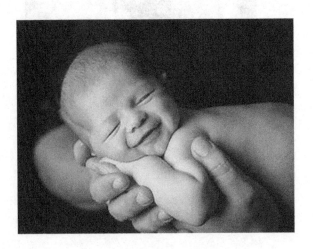

Maumivu: **pain, douleur**

Kupooza: **paralyzed, paralysé**

Mshipa: vein, veine

Mishipa: veins, veines

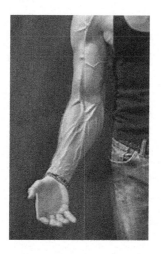

Saa ya kutembelea mgonjwa: visiting hour, heure de visite

Saa za kutembelea wagonjwa: visiting hours, heures de visite

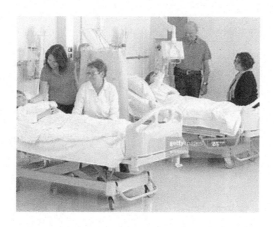

Tapika: vomit , vomir

Mtaalamu: specialist, spécialiste

Wataalamu: specialists, spécialistes

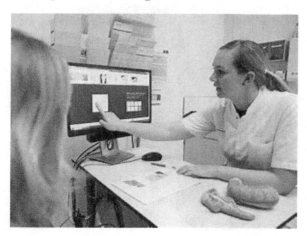

Ugonjwa wa baridi yabisi: arthritis, **arthrite**

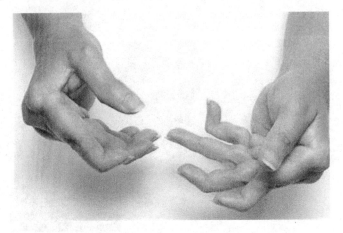

Mzio: allergy, **allergie**

Mzio: allergies, **allergies**

Kitu cha kufunga/kukazia: brace, attache

Vitu vya kufungia/kukazia: braces, attaches

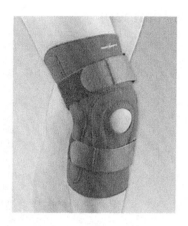

Tako/nyuma: breech, fesse

Matako/nyuma: breeches, fesses

Kansa: cancer, **cancer**

Kansa: cancers, **cancers**

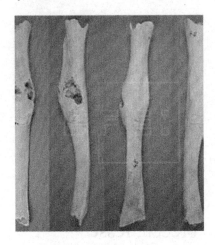

Kanisa dogo: chapel, **chapelle**

Makanisa madogo: chapels, **chapelles**

Hali mbaya: critical condition, état critique

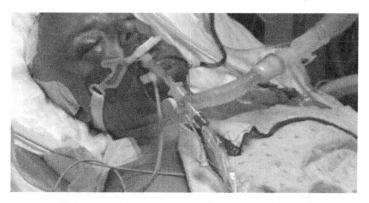

Upungufu wa maji: dehydrated, déshydraté

Kisukari: **diabetes, diabète**

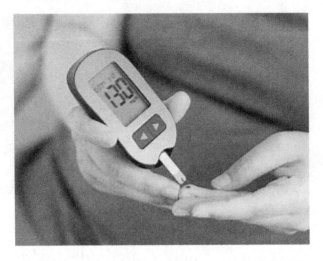

Adha/wasiwasi: **discomfort, gêne**

Homa: fever, fièvre

Mafua: flu, grippe

Mshtuko wa moyo: heart attack, **crise cardiaque**

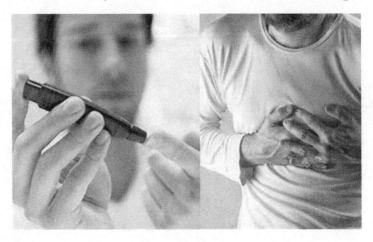

Virusi vya Ukimwi: HIV, **VIH**

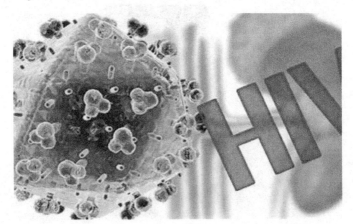

Ugonjwa: illness, maladie

Magonjwa: illnesses, maladies

Mtoto: child, enfant

Watoto: children, enfants

END
FIN